The Wild Dolphin Project:

Long-term Research of
Atlantic Spotted Dolphins
in the Bahamas

To Sarah,
  Keep up the great
interest in dolphins! Maybe
we will see you
out with us someday!

Dr. Denise L. Herzing

Denise L Herzing

WILD DOLPHIN PROJECT is grateful to the friends, colleagues, research
assistants and crew who have contributed photographs for this book.
We especially thank the following individuals:

Tim Barrett
Dr. Barbara Brunnick
Marsha Coates
Anne E.
Capt. Will Engleby
Laura Urian-Engleby
Dr. Denise Herzing
Dan Hoskins
Nicole Mader
Jessica Miles
Kelly Moewe
Capt. Peter Roberts
Bill Rossiter
Cindy Rogers
Diane Ross
Lynn Thomas
Patricia Weyer

Published by: THE WILD DOLPHIN PROJECT®

100% of the proceeds from the sale of this book go to support the work and research of the
WILD DOLPHIN PROJECT
P.O. Box 8436
Jupiter, FL 33468
wilddolphinproject@earthlink.net
www.WildDolphinProject.org

Manuscript: Dr. Denise L. Herzing
Copy-editor: Kelly Moewe and Jessica Miles
Designer: Jessica Miles and WDP staff

Printed and bound by Southeastern Printing/Blue Water Graphics

In memory of Dr. Kenneth Norris

Contents

...potted dolphins forage ...n the shallow sandbank ...or flounders and wrasse ...uried in the sand ...opposite page).

5

Preface

This book is an accumulation of many years of research and observation of one resident group of Atlantic spotted dolphins in the Bahamas. In 1984, as a young graduate student, I set out to find a location in the wild to study the life and communication system of wild dolphins. At the time, I was working in a captive facility, correlating the vocalization and behavior of four bottlenose dolphins. Although the research was interesting, I had set my mind to follow Jane Goodall's methods: find a location, commit to spending time, and allow the dolphins to become comfortable with our presence in the water. My goal was to document their lives over multiple generations, and record their interactions, sounds and behavior, in an attempt to decipher their communication system.

I was already familiar with the field of marine mammalogy. I had worked with gray whales and harbor seals in Oregon, humpback whales in the Caribbean, and bottlenose dolphins in California. What I was looking for was a site, in the wild, where a researcher could spend time in the water observing dolphins in their natural habitat. Somehow I knew it existed, but where? One night when I was living in San Francisco, I saw a television program called "In the Kingdom of Dolphins," produced by Hardy Jones. He had documented a site in the Bahamas where wild spotted dolphins could be approached and observed underwater. I had many questions including how often and how long could they be observed? Riveted with curiosity, I called Hardy. He generously agreed to let me view some of his old film to get a better sense of the research potential.

Simultaneously, Oceanic Society Expeditions, with whom I had researched gray whales, had decided to run ecotourism trips out to this site. The timing couldn't have been better! I volunteered to be their naturalist so that I could ascertain the research potential of the site. A longtime friend and roommate, Linda Castell, immediately recognized the stubborn determination in my eyes, and generously donated money for my first video system, with hydrophone input, to capture what I observed both visually and acoustically. Perseverance and support have carried me through the many years of funding challenges, boat nightmares, and research struggles. Since that first season in 1985, I have spent five months of every summer at sea, determined to observe whatever the dolphins would show me. I have remained ready and waiting, to make sense of what I saw to the best of my scientific abilities. Although the site was known from television, most scientists thought that it was unworthy of study, since the dolphins were "friendly." What I saw was the opposite. Researchers had done it with chimpanzees, elephants, and other social animals, why not with dolphins? I knew it could take a few decades, and few researchers are willing to bank their career on such slow progress.

This book is an attempt to share some basic aspects of the lives of this group of free-ranging dolphins. I am grateful to the many volunteers over the years, from Board members to boat crew. I am appreciative of many colleagues, especially the late Dr. Kenneth Norris, who understood the difficulties himself after working with spinner dolphins in Hawaii. He strongly supported and encouraged my bold adventure. I am indebted to my original mentors, Dr. Bruce Mate and Dr. Jim Sumich, who guided me through my early years as a scientist. Dr. Diana Reiss and Dr. Hal Markowitz were instrumental in my graduate work in San Francisco. The Board of Scientific Advisors also includes, Dr. Thomas White, Dr. Kenneth Pelletier, Dr. Christine Johnson, and Sir David Attenborough, who have all extended support and brought in new ideas to the project throughout the years. Other colleagues I would like to thank include, Dr. Whitlow Au, Dr. Ken Marten, Dr. Adam Pack, and Dr. Fabienne Delfour. My colleague, Dr. Barbara Brunnick struggled through early years of data analysis and processing with me and has greatly helped form the framework of this study.

I am also grateful to early funders including Cetacean Society International, the Whale and Dolphin Conservation Society, the American Cetacean Society, and individuals, including Dr. Linda Castell, Janice Miller, Richard Reitman, Elliot Levine, Carolyn Hay, Dr. Christopher Traughber, and William Stalcup, who helped get the Wild Dolphin Project on its own independent feet in 1988. Many thanks to Dan and Ro Sammis, David Schrenk, Will and Laura Engleby, Tim Barrett, Marsha Coates, Dan Hoskins, Peter Roberts, Nicole Mader, Kelly Moewe, Mindy Zuschlag, Kelly Rossbach, Judith Newby, Susan Bober, Stacey Beaulieu, Jessica Miles, NormaJeanne Byrd, Lynn Thomas, Suzanne Johnson, Bill O'Donell, Lynda Glennon, Diane Ross, Anne, Sarah, Nic, Ruth Petzold, Ivi Kimmel, Alice and Ed Crawford, Peyton Lee and Paul Jenkins, Lisa Fast, and Mac Hawley. Thanks to the Bahamas Department of Fisheries, Bahamas National Trust, Kent and Carol Landsberg Fd., the Henry Fd., the Seebe Fd., the Hawley Fd., the Plum Fd., the Geraldine R. Dodge Fd., Summerlee Fd., The Donald Slavik Family Fd., the Kenneth A. Scott Charitable Trust- a KeyBank Trust, the Shaklee Corporation, Iomega, Print Files, Kabana, Blue Water Graphics, Robin Makowski, Patricia Weyer, and to the many founders, volunteer cooks, first mates, and research assistants over the years.

Thank you all.

*One of the only
sexually dimorphic
traits between males
and females of this
species is the more
extreme white-tipped
rostrum males develop
with old age (opposite
page).*

The Wild Dolphin Project began as a dream of studying wild dolphins under water for a period of 20 years. The study began in 1985, when I arrived in the Bahamas for the first time. My research project was initially under the umbrella of the Oceanic Society Expeditions, a non-profit ecotour organization based in San Francisco. In 1988, irreconcilable differences between the ecotourism format and the research made it necessary to form my own non-profit organization, the Wild Dolphin Project. By that time, I had already accumulated photo-identifications and sexes of many of the spotted dolphins in the area, and my work with underwater video and sound continued. What changed in 1988 was the formation of a new entity that required some administration and coordination. Although the research has never changed from its original goals, various structural changes to the organization have occurred throughout the growth of the Wild Dolphin Project.

I continued my collection of identification marks, sexes, and visual and acoustic video, through the years. What many people don't realize is that these early years were critical in developing a trusting relationship with the dolphins that allows our continued observation. If you go to the Bahamas now, the dolphins appear naturally friendly and curious. However, it took about five years (1985-1990) for the dolphins to get comfortable with humans in the water, allowing us to observe their natural behavior. Throughout those early years, I focused on getting to know the individuals and let them seek us out when they wanted. In fact, I anchored the boat most of the time. I reasoned that if we placed ourselves in a regular location on the sandbank, the dolphins, being somewhat naturally curious, would seek us out. That is exactly what happened. The dolphins often came by our anchored vessel at regular times, during what I suspected was their "social" time, when they were perhaps free from foraging and baby-sitting duties so critical to their natural lives.

I also practiced hands off, non-invasive, respectful interaction, and reasoned that this respect was a long-term investment for the work. How could you expect to have a wild animal show you its world, if it was wary of you? If it had been successful for Jane Goodall and her observations of chimpanzees, why couldn't it work with dolphins? I now suspect that to some people this thought was a bit crazy. In these days of such advanced technology, most scientists want data and answers as quickly as possible. A lot of theory, with small amounts of data, seems to be the mode. But I felt strongly that the patient approach of mutual respect and appropriate etiquette would eventually pay off; five years later it did.

In 1990, the dolphins began to show us extensive aspects of their lives. We could swim along with them for hours and they went about their own business. To me this was perhaps an "old-school" naturalist approach because I remained patient and willing to immerse myself into the world of the nonhuman animal. I modeled my research after a true naturalist, Dr. Kenneth Norris, who let nature tell its own story and then checked it with the appropriate scientific methods. Since this approach is expensive and time consuming, the Wild Dolphin Project became a vehicle for supporting the research.

Our data collection routine, although modified somewhat over the years, has remained consistent. After every encounter with the dolphins, we log the location and environmental data, identify individuals, report total counts of age classes and sexes present, and log video and photographs. Meticulous logging and tracking of this diverse information has allowed us to maximize the information from every encounter. In addition, every evening we review the underwater video and log activity, individual identification marks, sounds, and video counter numbers. The Wild Dolphin Project has gathered thousands of photographs and hundreds of hours of underwater video. Without meticulous logging of such detail, current analysis of behavior and sound would

be impossible. With a vast long-term database, we can look back over the years and compare the behavior of multiple mothers and calves, or the development of male aggression. This investment in long-term data collection is critical for projects tracking multi-generation societies like dolphins.

1990 marked the first expansion of our study area. By that time, we had documented over 100 individuals in the group. Some were juveniles who would grow up in front of our eyes and have their own calves. Some were adults whom we still observe today, sometimes with the same alliances. Now that many individuals were familiar with us, we began moving around in their habitat. We wanted to document their range, movement, and the types of habitat in which they spent time. This was to be an important step in the growth of the Wild Dolphin Project. We began to see different types of foraging behavior that we had never previously observed while we were anchored. We saw bottlenose dolphins "crater" feeding for deeply buried fish and eels in nearby grassy areas. In 1991, we observed dolphins hunting on the deep edge of the sandbank where fish and squid amass at night. We observed types of reef fishing performed by bottlenose dolphins on the coral reefs. One of the most interesting observations we made was of the extensive and complex relationship that spotted dolphins have with the resident bottlenose dolphins in the area.

In 1991, I gave my first multimedia talk on the sound and behavioral work at the Marine Mammal conference in Chicago. I had been hesitant to present the work, due to concern of causing extensive human impact in the area. I would have preferred to keep the research location private in order to avoid the problem of more tourism boats and potentially invasive research that I believed might be harmful to our relationship with the dolphins. When I first began working in the Bahamas, I approached the Bahamian government about my concerns. With their blessing, I developed some voluntary guidelines for vessels in the area. Luckily, the impact of more ecotour boats and research has been minimal (most likely due to the offshore location).

After the 1991 conference, I began collaborating with other scientists, although I continued to stay away from any invasive methods. I have been committed to benign and non-invasive techniques from the beginning. I reasoned that interacting with another species, long-term, would involve a commitment to an appropriate interspecific ethic. To me, that meant "hands off" and non-disturbance to the best of our abilities. If the dolphins wanted to interact, we would take photographs of their spots, sex them, and observe whatever else they would show us.

If they wanted to leave, then we would let them, without following them or forcing ourselves upon them. "In their world, on their terms" has been, and continues to be, our motto, and scientifically it has paid off. With their growing comfort with us in the water, they began to ignore us, and the opportunity to observe their interactions with each other emerged.

The Wild Dolphin Project acquired its own research vessel in 1992, "*Stenella*," which we named after the dolphins. Our small dinghy was to be called "*frontalis*"; thus forming the name *Stenella frontalis*, the scientific name of the Atlantic spotted dolphin. Having our own research vessel greatly facilitated our work. We were able to control our research schedule, and began working in adjacent areas, like Bimini and the Abacos, in the winter to see if we could further extend the range of our observations. We also designed areas aboard the research vessel for research equipment and hosted collegial visits.

I was eager to expand our work with other expertise, but not at the dolphins' expense. Dr. Kenneth Norris was one of the first to join us and witnessed the incredible opportunity for observation and interaction. Dr. Whitlow Au, "Mr. Sonar" of the dolphin world, later joined us for some high-frequency sound acquisition work. Dr. Christine Johnson and I collaborated on some of the bottlenose/spotted interaction work. Finally in 1997, Dr. Adam Pack, Dr. Ken Marten, Dr. Diana Reiss, and Dr. Fabienne Delfour joined us for our new two-way communication project. Graduate students studied association patterns (Dr. Barbara Brunnick), developmental behavior (Kelly Moewe and Jessica Miles), bottlenose dolphins (Kelly Rossbach and Cindy Rogers), sound and behavior (Sylvan Oehan), signature whistles (Volker Deecke), burst-pulsed sounds (Michiel Schotten), and high-frequency sound collection (Marc Lammers).

Genetic work began in 1999, through the collection of fecal material in the water. For years, I had wanted to incorporate a genetic picture, which could give us a view of paternity and other details unattainable through observation. Through known paternities, we will be able to deduce the relatedness of every dolphin in our population, which will reveal how kin selection plays a part in the social structure of these dolphins. However, sampling their DNA has proven to be difficult until only recently. In the past, biopsy darting was the only way to obtain mitochondrial DNA. I decided to wait instead of risking the dolphins' trust. Dr. Hal Whitehead and others began working with sloughed off skin samples to determine genetic information of large whales. In our case, Kim Parsons (a graduate student in Scotland) approached us about collecting fecal materials from our bottlenose dolphins. She eventually refined the method substantially, to give us the genetic tools to obtain mitochondrial DNA from fecal samples collected from identified individuals in the water.

The Wild Dolphin Project has grown into a much broader research project over the years by incorporating other eager minds who kept consistent with the same ethics and concern for the dolphins' well being. As a faculty member at Florida Atlantic University (in Boca Raton, Florida), I have been able to take on graduate students to help with ongoing and future work. This remains the work of the Wild Dolphin Project today. We are now able to research new aspects of the lives of these dolphins, including reproductive rates, association patterns, GIS and habitat use, the development of behavior, movement between areas, feeding patterns, sound and behavioral correlation with individual personalities and sound use. This field site and relationship with the dolphins remains a unique and precious opportunity to illuminate their world in the wild.

In 1992 the Wild Dolphin Project acquired its own research vessel, a 20 meter power catamaran which was promptly named "Stenella" after the Latin species name (opposite page).

*Nursing:
Mothers and calves,
like Little Gash and her
first calf Little Hali,
are the most stable unit
in spotted dolphin
society. In 1985 Little
Gash was only a
juvenile, and as of
2002 she has had three
calves (opposite page).*

Taxonomy

When I first visited the Bahamas in 1985, little was known about this species. In fact, the taxonomy of spotted dolphins was quite messy. Now we know that spotted dolphins can have quite different coloration and spotted patterns and still are the same species. Originally called *Stenella plagiodon,* the species is now identified as *Stenella frontalis,* the Atlantic spotted dolphin. This species is only found in the Atlantic from one edge of the ocean to the other, in-between New Jersey, the Azores, and Venezuela. Other spotted dolphins exist, including the pantropical spotted dolphin (*Stenella attenuata*), an open ocean, large schooling species that lives in the Atlantic and Pacific Oceans. Recent genetic work actually places Atlantic spotted dolphins closer in relation to bottlenose dolphins (*Tursiops sp.*) than to other *Stenella* dolphins such as the spinner dolphin (*S. longirostris*), which is also found in tropical oceans.

Photo Identification

One of my first priorities was to document individuals by their natural marks. Photo identification has been used with many terrestrial species as well as with orcas in the Pacific Northwest. The idea is to find markings on an animal that are consistent and unique over the years. Although spotted dolphins have spots, they do not appear until they are a few years old. So my early days were spent using my underwater Nikonos camera, photographing and sexing as many individuals as possible.

In order to ensure successful photo identification, redocumenting animals over consecutive years is critical for tracking individuals. Marks, such as spots or gashes on the body can change slightly over time. Despite the popular misconception that only one photograph is necessary to identify a dolphin, it is particularly critical to photograph them every year to note these changes. We tracked whatever we could, including scars, spots, nicks in the fins and flukes, and coloration patterns. The calves were especially challenging. It was easy to lose the calves in our database if they reached the age of three without developing any spots or scars. Distinctive melon marks and throat coloration facilitated our abilities to monitor unspotted youngsters.

Fluke Nicks

Over time, dolphins can acquire distinctive fluke nicks and notches. Rosepetal (left) shows her ragged-edged fluke, and Little Gash (right) has one large notch out of the left side of her fluke.

Dorsal Nicks

Some dorsal fins have good identifying marks such as Geo's with its dramatic nicks (left), possibly the result of a shark attack, or Punchy's more subtle fin (right) that is split at the tip.

16

Other Nicks

Our underwater observations allow us to use full body marks for individual identifi cation like Little Gash's tail stock gash (left) and Ridgeway's notched peduncle (right), likely the result of entwinement with fishing line.

Spots and Body Marks

Although new spots are added over time, some marks, like Horseshoe's large black mark (left), and White Spot's obvious white mark (right), have remained consistent over the years.

17

Dr. William Perrin originally described age class categories for Pantropical spotted dolphins. These categories have been modified and tracked on this population of Atlantic spotted dolphins since 1985. Individuals are photographed through all color phases including two-tones (calves, top left), speckleds (juveniles, top right), mottleds (young adults, bottom left), and fused (old adults, bottom right).

Sexing

Sexing dolphins can be challenging. All genitalia are internal, and Atlantic spotted dolphins are not very sexually dimorphic (i.e. males and females do not look that different from each other). To sex spotted dolphins, we depend upon their close proximity in the water so that we can see their external slits when they turn inverted. Females have two mammary slits on either side of one genital slit, while males have one long genital slit and one anal slit. Over the years we have sexed and reverified our entire community of spotted dolphins.

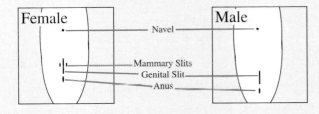

Age Classes

Detailed documentation of 220 individuals over the past 18 years has yielded important information on the lives and reproductive habits of Atlantic spotted dolphins. Tracking individuals, and following their lives, as they pass through four distinct age related stages of pigmentation, has been critical to this work (left). Long-term life histories and relationships are tracked using underwater photographs.

Gender identification is possible when the dolphins present their ventral areas. Females (top) are identified by a division sign arrangement of their slits with the two mammary slits located on either side of the genital slit. The males (bottom) have an exclamation point arrangement with an elongated genital slit line leading down to the anus (See diagram to left).

19

Calves (Two-Tones), Age 1-3

When spotted dolphins are born they have no spots. Instead, they resemble young bottlenose dolphins with their "two-toned," gray and white coloration. Calves are usually born in the spring and fall with fetal folds and little knowledge of the ocean. Calves are about 1/4 the size (90cm) of their mothers. During the first year of life, over 25% of calves are lost, most likely due to natural health problems as well as predation from sharks. If the calf survives, it spends most of its time with its mother, although it is exposed to the mother's friends and other calves throughout this period. Over the first three years, the calf will nurse, but will also learn to catch fish, especially flounder, which can easily be snagged off the bottom. Calves can be quite precocious and soon learn how to play and cavort with other calves in the nursery group. Since the mother associates with other females with calves, young dolphins have plenty of exposure to their peers at an early age. It is not unusual for one- and two-year old calves to be tended by juveniles when their mothers are out of visual range. By age 3, calves usually have at least a few spots on their ventral surface.

Juveniles (Speckled), Age 4-8

By age 4, the young "speckled" dolphin usually gains a younger sibling and is therefore no longer the main focus of its mother. Juveniles have spots on their ventral side and now begin to develop white spots on their dorsal surface. Their main social groups are composed of other juveniles, many of whom they know from their "two-tone" years. Young juveniles are playful and exploratory and are often the victims of shark attacks. They display behavior, including mock fights and mating. A predominant activity associated with this age class is baby-sitting younger calves. Mothers often venture off to forage and leave their calves with male or female juveniles. While speckleds tend to be fiercely independent, they are an intricate part of the larger dolphin group and continue to associate with their mothers, siblings, and other members of the dolphin society.

Knowing the players, and their relationships as they progress through the four age classes, is a priority in the work (opposite page).

BAHAMIAN ATLANTIC SPOTTED DOLPHIN
AGE CLASSES AND PIGMENTATION PATTERNS

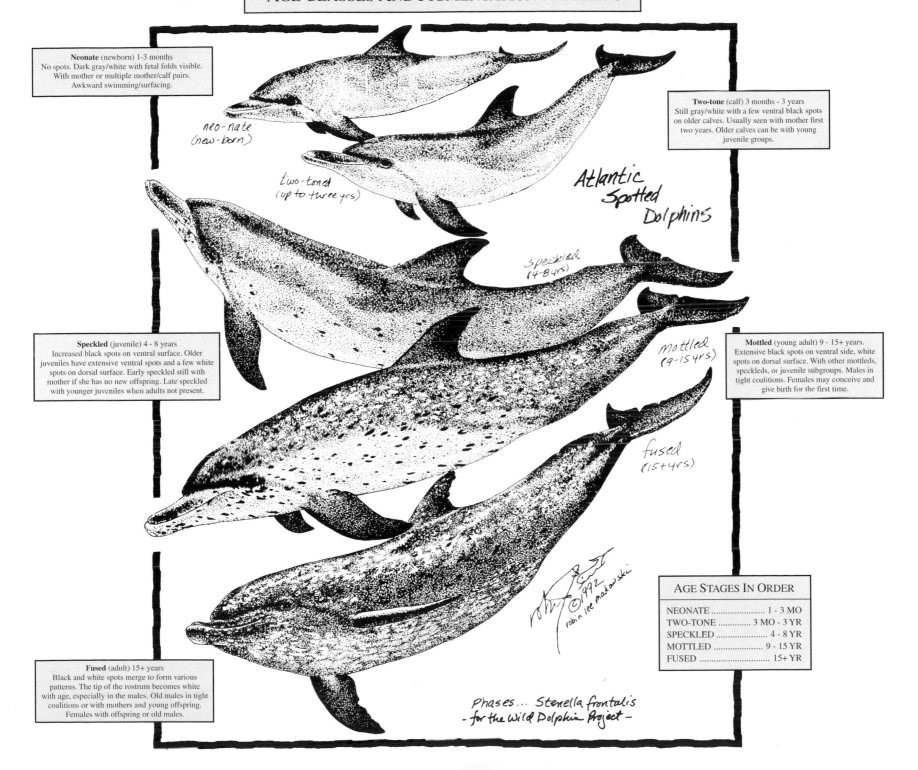

Neonate (newborn) 1-3 months
No spots. Dark gray/white with fetal folds visible.
With mother or multiple mother/calf pairs.
Awkward swimming/surfacing.

neo-nate (new-born)

Two-tone (calf) 3 months - 3 years
Still gray/white with a few ventral black spots
on older calves. Usually seen with mother first
two years. Older calves can be with young
juvenile groups.

two-toned (up to three yrs)

Atlantic Spotted Dolphins

speckled (4-8 yrs)

Speckled (juvenile) 4 - 8 years
Increased black spots on ventral surface. Older
juveniles have extensive ventral spots and a few white
spots on dorsal surface. Early speckled still with
mother if she has no new offspring. Late speckled
with younger juveniles when adults not present.

mottled (9-15 yrs)

Mottled (young adult) 9 - 15+ years.
Extensive black spots on ventral side, white
spots on dorsal surface. With other mottleds,
speckleds, or juvenile subgroups. Males in
tight coalitions. Females may conceive and
give birth for the first time.

fused (15+ yrs)

©1992 robin lee makowski

Fused (adult) 15+ years
Black and white spots merge to form various
patterns. The tip of the rostrum becomes white
with age, especially in the males. Old males in tight
coalitions or with mothers and young offspring.
Females with offspring or old males.

AGE STAGES IN ORDER

NEONATE	1 - 3 MO
TWO-TONE	3 MO - 3 YR
SPECKLED	4 - 8 YR
MOTTLED	9 - 15 YR
FUSED	15+ YR

*Phases... Stenella frontalis
- for the Wild Dolphin Project -*

Females can appear visibly pregnant during our field season. Katy gave birth to Kai, our first "3rd generation" calf, in 1999 (top). Newborn calves stay close to their mothers, (bottom).

Young Adults (Mottled), Age 9-15

Young adults are labeled as "mottled" because of the development of mottled patterns of white spots on their dorsal area and continued black spot proliferation over their entire bodies. It is at this age when females become sexually mature and become pregnant. Courtship and mating behavior become more frequent and serious. Females mature and give birth for the first time around the age of 9 or 10. Pregnancy (gestation) lasts about one year, and first parturition females experience varying degrees of survivorship of their first offspring. Although behaviorally and sexually active, it is unknown when male Atlantic spotted dolphins reach sexual maturity. It is during the young adult phase that males form strong alliances to herd and court females. Like other dolphins, males may mature later than the females of their own species. With future genetic research, this is one of the many questions that we will be able to answer.

Old Adults (Fused), Age 15 and older

Older adults can be recognized by the extensive black and white spotting that covers their entire body. In many cases, spots merge and coalesce to form contrasting dark and light areas, hence the term "fused." By the time they reach this age, a female may have had 2-3 offspring. They continue to reproduce, and in some cases reproduce even while they are already grandmothers. Many of the adult females we met in 1985 (e.g. Luna, Gemini) continue to give birth every three to four years. From our estimates of age class, these females are estimated to be at least 35 to 40 years old. We don't know how long females continue to reproduce, or if they have post-reproductive years solely as grandmothers (like orcas). To date, all of our adult females are producing offspring.

Males of this age continue to display their long-term friendships with other males, although some relationships can fluctuate depending on dominance changes or death. Adult males are the most elusive age class of the group. They can be seen on peripheral areas of the study site, and may take on a sentry role while perhaps mating with females in adjacent areas to ensure genetic diversity. Many old males we know (e.g. Romeo, Big Gash) have been fused since 1985, and we can extrapolate from this information that they are 35 or 40 years old.

Second only to the bond between mother and calf, males also form life-long bonds (top). Calves often swim with their head near the mother's mammary glands (bottom).

23

Color

General body coloration can be contrasting, as with Dos who has a clear separation between a light dorsal and a dark ventral side, (left) or consistent as with Summer's light appearance (right).

Throat Marks

Young dolphins sometimes have "throat straps" that allow individual identification and tracking.

Melon Marks

Distinct melon marks are usually a bit different on the left and right side of a dolphins head, but still make individual identification easier.

Eye Marks & Underbites

Raccoon (left), a juvenile male, has dark eye lines that stand out in the water. Some dolphins have dramatic underbites (right) that also aid identification.

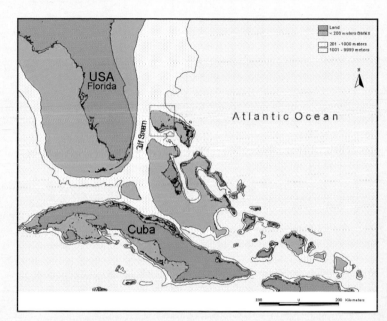

aeial view of "Stenella" ar the edge of the shallow ndbanks and deep water pposite page).

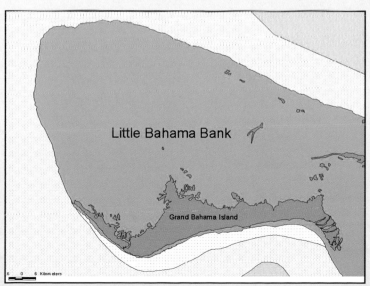

The Seasons

You might expect that after nearly two decades of study, we would understand all the habits and movements of a resident group of dolphins, but working at sea has its challenges. Our main field season is May through September, which ironically is hurricane season. The rest of the year the sandbank is exposed to the northeast storms that move along the Atlantic coast. This makes if very difficult to engage in any regular work in the winter. While the summer months may bring hurricanes, the weather is best at this time unless there is a big storm nearby. So we still wonder if the dolphins stay in the study site during the winter months. If they do, does their behavior and diet remain consistent throughout the year?

The shallow sandbanks of the Bahamas provide a unique habitat for Atlantic spotted dolphins. Shallow and safe white sand and reefs are available for daytime activity, while access to the deep water edge provides nighttime fishing on the deep-scattering layer. Foraging at night in deep water, dolphins live in a primarily acoustic world.

A peaceful sunrise in the morning (left) can lead to a day where large anvil clouds develop (right), hinting of afternoon thunderstorms to come.

Typical tropical weather in the summer may include squalls (left) that quickly pass, allowing us to catch the beautiful sunsets over the ocean (right).

Summer is our main field season, a time when water clarity and warmth is at its best (left). Passing storms provide shade and coolness during the hot Bahamian summer days (right).

Tropical summers also include water-spouts (left) and hurricanes, so we must be vigilant in monitoring developing weather patterns. We also track tidal flux influenced by the moon (right).

29

Equipment in the Field and Lab

The most remarkable feature of this study site is the ability to view these dolphins underwater and in close proximity. Spotted dolphins display surface activity, but to accurately interpret behavior, we prioritize our work to an underwater venue.

My priority in the water has always been to document and interpret the communication system of these dolphins. The framework for this interpretation is in knowing individuals, their relationships, and the basic contexts of their lives. Because of the dolphin's extended acoustic world, we need special equipment to hear, record, and document their lives.

Although taking notes underwater seems like a good idea, it is not a practical method of data collection for fast moving dolphins. The best we can do is record behavior on video tape to review later, in slow motion. With the help of a computer, a review of sound recordings help determine details of their behavior. Colleagues join us both in the field and lab to help collect and analyze special data including high frequency sounds and patterns of signature whistles.

We use both the underwater video and still photography to verify identifications and document behavior. The human eye is crucial for the collection of other information. We rely on our training and abilities as observers to track individuals as they are engaged in behavior. This

is critical for understanding the lives of dolphins and in the interpretation of these data. In the lab we use computers, sound processing equipment, and organizational skills to track the long-term slide, video, and sound database.

Crucial to our work is the recording of simultaneous sound and underwater video (top). We have recorded the underwater behavior and vocalizations of many individuals and correlated the sounds with observable underwater behavior. In our Florida laboratory, still images are analyzed using photo identification techniques (bottom).

Living in a predominately acoustic world, dolphins may close their eyes when sleeping or resting, listening for any dangers that may be approaching (opposite page).

Large dolphin groups are often observed moving along the ocean bottom in formation, sometimes scanning for buried fish.

Groups and Movement on the Sandbank

The 220 spotted dolphins in the area tend to divide themselves up into three groups that I call the North, Central, and South groups. Of course, animals are always more complicated then we initially think. Although the three groups are distinct, Flying A, a Central female, disappeared for two years and appeared in the South group with her first calf, KP. Tilloo, who was in the South group, has managed to cover the entire range, and finally joined the Central group.

What Dr. Barbara Brunnick and I discovered, after some data analysis, was actually quite simple. Females, although faithful to tighter ranges than the males, can change groups and associations by reproductive status alone. All dolphins display tight friendships, but females are driven by similar or changing reproductive status. Perhaps they bond due to safety concerns, or they may join together because they need similar types and quantities of food when pregnant.

The males are quite different. Second only to the regular bond between mothers and calves, males form life-long friendships. They survey the entire area, looking for females and sometimes younger males join their coalitions. In fact, their ranges may be even

larger than we see, since we are seasonal migrants to the area. New genetic work in adjacent areas may shed light on the genetic dispersal both within and between these groups of spotted dolphins.

Living Sea and Sky

The islands of the Bahamas are surrounded by rings of living coral (left). Soaring overhead are frigate birds (right), and their presence in the sky often indicates that dolphins are nearby.

Rays and Sharks

A stingray's outline is seen on the white sandy bottom (left). Nurse sharks (right) are often observed resting on the reefs and wrecks on the banks.

Sharks

Both bottlenose and spotted dolphins are prey to multiple species of sharks that inhabit the sandbank and deep, offshore waters nearby. Tiger sharks (*Galeocerdo cuvieri*), bull sharks (*Carcharhinus leucas*), and scalloped hammerhead sharks (*Sphyrna lewini*) are the most commonly observed species in our study site. Tiger sharks are seen most frequently in the spring and fall, when young dolphin calves are born and are the most vulnerable. Tigers reach over 5 meters in length and, although cautious in nature, are still impressive in the water to a human researcher. Bull sharks are not as large as tigers, and are a robust and bold species, following and bumping humans as well as dolphins. Large hammerheads are often sighted, but they are usually in search of stingrays on the bottom.

Sharks, like other animals on the sandbank, have an important niche as one of the top predators of the food web. They have, no doubt, been a strong force in the evolution of dolphin intelligence. Strategies for protection and escape from sharks include fleeing, remaining motionless on the bottom, or chasing the shark away.

Large sharks, including tiger sharks (top) are regularly seen on the sandbank. Hammerhead, bull, and nurse sharks are also found in the area. In 1991, Nassau, as a two-year-old, received a large bite from a shark in the area (bottom). In this attack she also lost the tip of her dorsal fin. Although large, the wound was shallow, and she is currently the mother of a two-year-old calf.

Although juveniles, are the most likely to receive shark-bites (top), mothers like Luna are also vulnerable when they are caring for their young calves (bottom left). Large bottlenose dolphins like Nose, an adult female, have been attacked (bottom right).

Remoras and Other Hazards

Large purple remoras, <u>Remora australis</u>, attach to dolphins, especially those with skin problems or wounds. Martin, a young male calf, suffered terribly during this tenant's stay (top).

As in other parts of the world, dolphins may be impacted by human activities. Dash, a young adult male, was seen with fishing wire wrapped around his tailstock that eventually began cutting through (bottom).

Remoras are thought to be a harmless annoyance as they attach to the dolphins, some remaining for years. Most likely, remoras are harvesting food in the water that the dolphins swim through and perhaps feed on sloughed skin. We have observed remoras on dolphins with fresh wounds actively working around the injured area. This species of remora, *Remora australis*, is specific to whales and dolphins. Another hitchhiker is the small, stalked barnacle, *Xenobalanus sp.*, that is often attached to a fluke or dorsal fin and hitches a temporary ride. Although harmless, this small organism can be mistaken by uninformed swimmers as a "tag," thought to be put there by inquiring scientists (far from the truth).

Humans are an influential component in the ocean's ecosystem. Hazardous human impacts include fishing line entanglements, dumping of plastic waste products that may be mistaken for prey, and accumulation of toxins, such as PCB's, that adhere to the fat or blubber of the dolphins. These toxins may then be passed on to offspring, causing birth defects and death. Although we have not observed any dead dolphins in our study site (bodies are difficult to find in the open ocean), we have seen older dolphins who were emaciated. Dolphins also suffer from typical mammalian problems, including fungal, viral, and bacterial infections.

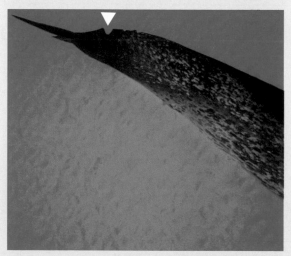

External Parasites

Martin's skin condition shows how remoras may leave behind signs of their presence (left). Stalked barnacles, Xenobalanus sp., attach to the fins and flukes of dolphins, hitching a temporary ride (right).

Viral and Fungal Infections

Bottlenose dolphins are sometimes seen with "lobomycosis," a contagious fungus (left). Some spotted dolphins show evidence of various fungal, viral, and bacterial infections such as pox or tatoo virus (right).

Names, Individuals, and Generations

Social behavior, including touch, is used to solidify bonds and reassure excited youngsters. Here, a pec to pec rub is observed ("pec" is short for pectoral fin) (opposite page).

During the early years, I named spotted dolphins mnemonically according to physical features to trigger my memory. Some had obvious gashes and earned names like "Big Gash" and "Little Gash." This is a technique used in the field to enable quick recall. I chose to name our individuals, rather than give them numbers. Not only is it easier to remember names instead of numbers, but, like Jane Goodall and other long-term researchers, I believe that nonhuman beings each have their own personality and deserve names. In the water, it is necessary to quickly identify individuals by their marks. Later, as relationships between spotted dolphins became more clear, I began naming offspring with the first letter of their mothers name and also sometimes used themes. For example, Rosemole is a female I've known since 1985, and she had her first offspring Rosebud in 1991, Rosepetal in 1994, and Rozita in 1999. Snowflake's family includes Snow, Sleet, Slush, and Storm. Snowflake became a grandmother in 2000 when Snow, her daughter, gave birth to her first son, Sunami. The tracking of lineages is critical to understanding relationships over the long-term and is essential in understanding dolphin society.

The reality of fieldwork is that many challenges emerge over the years. For example, one might have the right side of a dolphin on film for years without getting a shot of the left side. Luckily, because of my focus on sound and behavior from the beginning, I have used underwater video as a tool. Such equipment has the advantage of continuous shots of the same dolphins, to enable the researcher to verify the right and left side of an individual.

Other tracking issues have emerged. If a dolphin is not photographed during a given field season or two, by the time another shot is taken, the individual has gained so many spots that it is not easily matched. Luckily, because we use the whole body and many features for matching, we have been able to look backwards in our database. We discovered that a fused female named Dos is actually a female named Jumper, who was identified in the early 80s and whom we thought had disappeared. Dr. Barbara Brunnick and other students on the team do this meticulous tracking in the lab. They diligently review and organize slides for double and triple checks.

This is the demand of the science, to recheck and verify through repeated steps. The photo-identification process is critical to every research aspect, such as sound and behavioral analysis, and is the long-term framework for the Wild Dolphin Project.

Third Generation Dolphin Families

Female spotted dolphins begin reproducing around the age of 9 or 10. Adult females like Snowflake and Paint, who we have observed since the 1980s, are now grandmothers. Their two families represent the first third generation groups in our dolphin community. Notice that both Snowflake and Paint are simultaneously mothers and grandmothers, and their offspring are the uncles and aunts of their grandchildren. Like primate and elephant societies, multi-generational dolphin societies have complex relationships, communication, and learning skills.

THE SNOW FAMILY

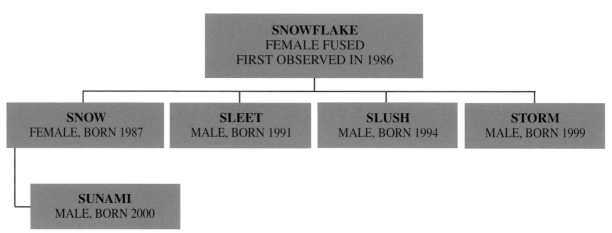

SNOWFLAKE
FEMALE FUSED
FIRST OBSERVED IN 1986

SNOW
FEMALE, BORN 1987

SLEET
MALE, BORN 1991

SLUSH
MALE, BORN 1994

STORM
MALE, BORN 1999

SUNAMI
MALE, BORN 2000

THE PAINT FAMILY

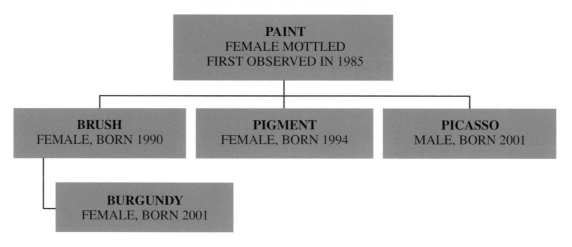

PAINT
FEMALE MOTTLED
FIRST OBSERVED IN 1985

BRUSH
FEMALE, BORN 1990

PIGMENT
FEMALE, BORN 1994

PICASSO
MALE, BORN 2001

BURGUNDY
FEMALE, BORN 2001

Tracking Associations

Over the years we have tracked associations between individuals in our group. Clearly, the strongest bond is between a mother and calf for the first three years of the calf's life. The second strongest association is between males. Punchy and Big Wave have been friends since 1985 and continue to associate as adults through 2002. These are long-term alliances critical to the protection and survival of the group and the mating success of individual males within the alliances.

Females exhibit strong friendships as well, but these friendships tend to fluctuate as their reproductive status changes. For example, three juveniles I've known since 1985 (Little Gash, Rosemole, and Mugsy), have exhibited strong degrees of associations through their juvenile years. When Rosemole and Mugsy became pregnant during the late 80s, they continued their friendship, but left Little Gash to mingle with other juveniles. Rosemole and Mugsy then formed new associations with other pregnant females or mothers with young calves. As their reproductive cycles caught up with each other, all three friendships were reestablished, but never to the same level as their juvenile period. Interestingly, some of their offspring currently have strong friendships, heralding in another cycle of sisterhood and brotherhood.

The Snow family (top). We are now seeing our first third generation of dolphin families. Grandmother Snowflake accompanies her daughter Snow and her grandson Sunami. Storm is Snowflake's new calf, making Sunami Storm's nephew... testimony to the multi-generational interactions in dolphin society.

Girlfriends, Little Gash and Rosemole (bottom) were close associates as juveniles. They spent little time with each other when Little Gash became pregnant, but, when their reproductive cycles were again in synch, they began associating once more.

41

Dolphins create sound through the vibration of tissue in their nasal passages. Sounds are focused through the melon, a fatty structure that focuses sound. Highly directional clicks are sent out and bounce off a target. Reflections are received through another fatty channel in the lower jaw and are transmitted to the inner ear. Dolphins have a typical mammalian inner ear, which processes sounds much like humans, however with some variation for higher and lower frequencies.

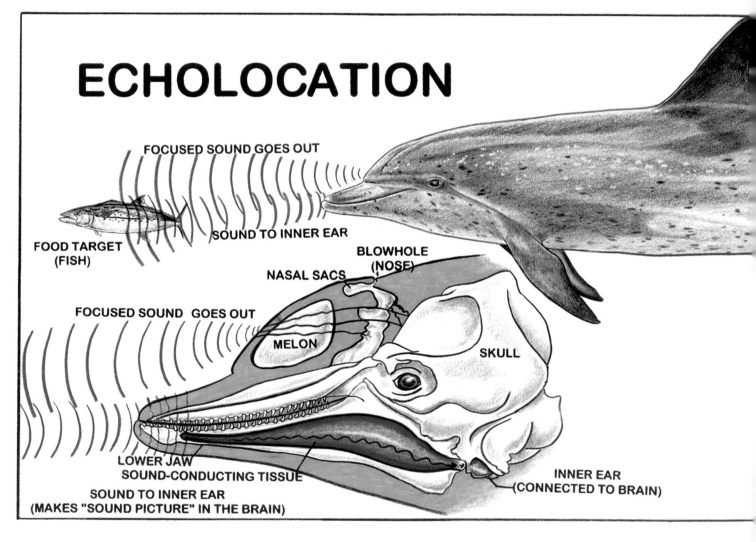

ECHOLOCATION

FOCUSED SOUND GOES OUT

FOOD TARGET (FISH)

SOUND TO INNER EAR

NASAL SACS

BLOWHOLE (NOSE)

FOCUSED SOUND GOES OUT

MELON

SKULL

LOWER JAW SOUND-CONDUCTING TISSUE

SOUND TO INNER EAR (MAKES "SOUND PICTURE" IN THE BRAIN)

INNER EAR (CONNECTED TO BRAIN)

How to Read a Spectrogram

Spectrograms are a visual representation of sound in the time/frequency domain. They are read left to right, with frequency (pitch) on the vertical axis and time on the horizontal axis. Intensity (loudness) is represented by the brightness of the sound. Until recently, most sounds have been recorded within human audible range. It is very likely that these sounds have ultrasonic components.

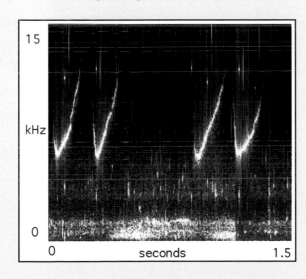

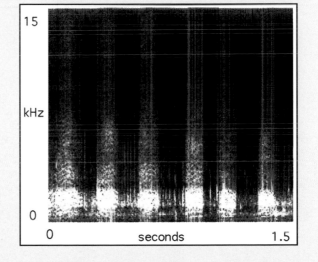

The spectrogram above shows the signature whistle of White Patches. The ascending and descending contour line indicates that the whistle is going up and down in pitch. These whistles are like a unique "name" produced by individual dolphins.

Burst-pulsed sounds are labeled as grunts, moans, or squawks. Although burst-pulses are more common than whistles in most dolphins' repertoires, how these sounds are used in the wild remains a mystery.

Bubbles

Bubbles are often released from the blowhole when a signature whistle is emitted. This helps us identify who created the individually unique whistle (left). Specific bubbles, such as a torus ring (right) communicate annoyance, draw attention, and help to herd fish.

Postural Communication

The use of postural communication such as an inverted stance with open mouths (left) and vertical stance behaviors (right) show how important vision is to a social being in clear water.

Some of the discoveries we have made over the years include the existence of signature whistles of individual dolphins, how whistles and other sounds are used, and basic correlations of sound to behavior.

Types of Dolphin Sounds

Dolphins make three different types of sound: Whistles, burst-pulsed, and echolocation. The first two are used primarily in social contexts, and the latter for hunting and navigating. But, it turns out that there is much overlap in the use of these sounds. But all sounds are produced and projected by the same mechanism. Examples of the three types of sounds and their correlated behaviors are as follows:

Whistles - Frequency-modulated whistles are known to travel for miles and are primarily used for contact and reunions between individuals. Each dolphin has its own characteristic signature whistle. These whistles are relatively stable over time and their spectrograms are unique even to the human eye. We hear signature whistles when mothers and calves are reuniting, during baby-sitting activities, and in courtship.

Burst-Pulsed - These sounds are used in close proximity interactions. In Atlantic spotted dolphins, we hear these sounds most frequently during fighting and aggressive activity. Commonly called squawks, moans, and blats, they are short in duration and intense in amplitude.

Echolocation - Echolocation clicks are used primarily in navigation and prey detection, however there may also be a social use to these sounds. Known to extend into the higher frequencies (up to 140 kHz for Atlantic spotted dolphins), human ears only hear components in the lower frequency range (<20 kHz).

Behavioral Correlation of Sound

Although many people think of dolphins as primarily acoustic creatures, spotted dolphins in clear waters use other modalities to communication, including postural signals, tactile signals, and possibly chemical signals. This multi-modal system of communication is typical of social mammals and allows for complexity and diversity. General descriptions of behavior and the correlated sounds are as follows.

An adult female, White Patches, supervises a youngster practicing catching a fish in the sand (top).

Dolphins also learn to snag needlefish at the surface (bottom).

Foraging

Typical types of foraging behavior include scanning for bottom fish, crater feeding, and chasing schooling fish. Extensive echolocation trains are usually observed with these behaviors.

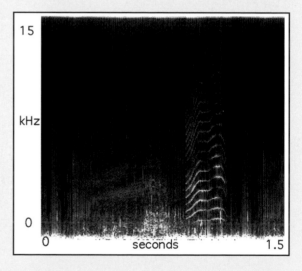

Echolocation clicks, or sonar, function to help dolphins detect and capture prey items. Slow click trains are observed as a dolphin approaches an object. Within a meter of capture, clicks are produced at rapid rate, called a terminal buzz.

Aggression

When dolphins fight they use a series of postures including head to head positions, open-mouth threats and body arches. Squawks are the most common sounds observed during aggressive behavior.

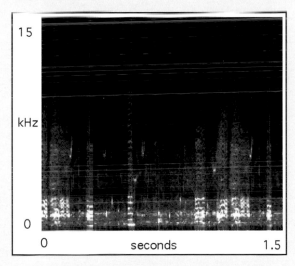

Squawks are broad-band, burst-pulsed sounds ranging from 0.2-12 kHz and higher, extending from 0.2-1.0 second, and with 200-1200 clicks per second. These sounds occur during agonistic and aggressive encounters as well as in sexual play activities. Squawks are emitted by both males and females as well as by all age classes.

Squawks, a type of burst-pulsed signal, are typically heard during aggressive behavior. Multiple dolphins may synchronize their squawks and their physical behavior during escalated fights. Head to head behaviors and open mouths are other common signs of aggression (top and bottom).

Dolphins often orient their rostra to the genital area of another dolphin, especially preceding mating behavior (top).

Dolphin courtship is very ritualized. Males approach females in inverted postures. As they approach they emit a genital buzz, that may either stimulate or serve to inspect the female upon approach. Copulation occurs belly to belly, with the male underneath. It is brief but may be repetitive and sometimes involves multiple males with one female.

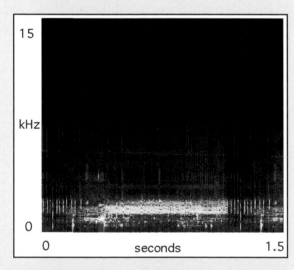

The male is typically underneath the female during mating behavior. White Spot, a male, is inverted underneath Venus, a female (bottom).

Genital buzzes are a high-repetition rate click train (1.2-2.5 kHz) with most energy in the lower frequencies, focused at the female during courtship. At 8-2000 clicks per second, they have also been observed during mother/calf discipline by both spotted and bottlenose dolphins.

Traveling and Resting

Dolphins are generally quiet during both resting and traveling. When spotted dolphins rest, they glide slowly underwater, often in close proximity, with one eye partially shut. When traveling in large groups, dolphins on the edge may occasionally vocalize when regrouping the pod, or during peripheral squabbles, but movement is usually quiet and organized.

Discipline and Baby-sitting

Mothers often discipline calves at an early age, as young dolphins face many risks at sea. Typically, a mother will hold a calf down on the bottom, or round it up from his playmates, if they are getting into trouble. Young dolphins will push the limits of parental tolerance, just like humans, and mothers set critical boundaries for behavior!

Surface versus Underwater

In most field studies, researchers identify and observe dolphins from the surface. The world's oceans, other than the tropics, do not afford underwater observation. The Bahamas provide a unique opportunity for researchers to study dolphins underwater on a regular basis, proving critical to the interpretation of their communication signals and behavior.

Latitude, Havana, and friend lazily float in the water column as they rest during mid-day (top).

Lilly nudges her son Leo's genital region (bottom), sometimes stimulating an erection. Sexual behavior such as this is thought to be social and quite normal in this tactile society.

49

Surface versus Underwater Observations

Simultaneous underwater observations reveal that, in some cases, aerial leaps can mean that a fight is occurring underwater (top).

In fact, dolphins escape to the surface not only to breath but to potentially reposition themselves for reentry to engage their opponent in head to head, aggressive behavior (bottom).

Aerial Behavior

Atlantic spotted dolphins display a variety of aerial behaviors, including breaches, back flips (left), and porpoising (right). At first glance leaping may look playful, but leaps may also be used to shed remoras and parasites, or to chase fish.

Bowriding

When bowriding, dolphins experience a free push by the water forced ahead of the bow (left). Spotted dolphins are very adept at bowriding upside down, perhaps giving them a look through the water's surface at the eager human observers (right).

51

Lazy days on the shallow sandbanks of the Bahamas allow rest, socializing and snacking on bottom fish (opposite page).

Since the initiation of our study, we have been able to observe spotted dolphins underwater every summer for 5 months. In the early years of this study, I always anchored in one location on the sandbank. I reasoned that if the dolphins became comfortable with us, they would be more willing to let us peer into their world. The fact is, our study would be nothing if the dolphins didn't allow us to tag along. We are slow and clumsy in the water, and if the dolphins leave, there is no way to catch up with them. This makes the work mutual and participatory. We respect their lives and time, and just try to be there when they are willing to show us something.

Over the years, we began expanding our study area to increase our behavioral observations. This led to new discoveries in their daily and nighttime activities.

Diurnal and Nocturnal Foraging Behavior

The shallow (5-15 m) sandbanks of the Bahamas are extremely diverse and productive areas. Although initially hidden from the human observer, many fish and crustacean species hide under the sand. The dolphins exploit these prey on a regular basis during the day. Flounder, razorfish, snake and conger eels, and other types of fish await the skilled dolphins who can echolocate under the sand. Most of the day is spent traveling around the shallows, snacking on bottom fish, resting, and socializing. Also, when the tide is right, schooling fish such as needlefish and ballyhoo are the targets of both dolphins and frigate birds. The shallow sandbanks are also good protection from large, oceanic predators. At least in the shallows, dolphins can swim along the bottom, or easily distinguish a predator against the bottom. Anyone who has jumped into deep water is familiar with the insecure feeling of the possibility of large creatures lurking in the depths. Dolphins experience the same issues. Shallow is safe, and deep is dangerous (but sometimes necessary for feeding).

At night, spotted dolphins often amass in larger groups and leave the shallow sandbanks, heading for the edge that meets deep water. In some areas along the edge, depths drop to 300 m., within 1.8 km of the sandbank, This extreme sloping edge draws fish, squid and dolphins who spend their nocturnal hours drifting with the north current on the edge while foraging.

53

Mysteries of Dolphin Sound and Behavior

One of the most striking findings about dolphin life in the wild is how much of the time dolphins are actually quiet. It turns out that they listen as well as produce sound. Sound may be used more selectively than we had previously assumed, and it may be more efficient to listen for predators and ocean noise than to continuously scan for such things.

Another challenge for researchers in the study of sound is in the recording of the full range, or bandwidth, of sound. Only recently, with the digital revolution, have systems been developed that show us their ultrasonic range. For many years, we haven't been able to hear or record these sounds that are above our human hearing range.

The final challenge in deciphering dolphin communication is the understanding of their society. Each dolphin is an individual, with varying relationships and histories. All these factors are critical for the interpretation of communication signals. Until we unravel more details of their lives, including which males sire offspring and if they migrate to other adjacent areas during the winter, we will never fully understand their lives. The Bahamas provide a unique opportunity to witness and describe dolphin life, society, and communication in the wild.

Dolphins continue to intrigue us... their communication and societal complexities remain in the realm of mystery.

Bottlenose Dolphins

Bottlenose dolphins, (*Tursiops truncatus*) also inhabit these waters and overlap territory with the spotted dolphins. Since 1985, over 200 bottlenose dolphins have been individually identified in the same areas as spotted dolphins. Kelly Rossbach, a graduate student from Oregon State University, meticulously identified all of these dolphins through many months of intense fieldwork. In addition, we have been able to track individual bottlenose dolphins throughout the entire area of Little Bahama Bank by working with Ken Balcomb and Diane Claridge, who monitor the far east end of the study area. The bottlenose dolphins often engage in a form of foraging we termed "crater" feeding, because of the telltale crater left in the sand after digging. Tasty morsels such as conger eels and razorfish are retrieved after crater feeding. Although spotted dolphins also dig in the sand, they tend to dig away from grass beds where bottlenose dolphin focus most of their foraging. The two species do not appear to have a high element of overlap in their foraging strategies.

One of the most remarkable social relationships observed at our study site is that between spotted and bottlenose dolphins on the sandbank. We see bottlenose dolphins and

Bottlenose dolphins are one meter larger than spotted dolphins and in general are individual foragers. Bottlenose dolphins spend much of their time on the sandbank cruising the bottom and digging for small fish (bottom). When digging deep, they leave a large "crater" in the sand.

55

spotted dolphins interacting with each other during 15% of our encounters. The majority of time (60%) these two cetacean species are engaged in traveling, playing, or resting together. Only a small percentage of time (5%) is spent foraging together, and even then, they feed on different food items. 35% of the time the two species are engaged in aggressive activities with each other. Bottlenose dolphins in this area are almost one meter larger than the adult spotted dolphins, so they can easily physically dominate the spotted dolphins. They charge, hit, and strike spotted dolphins, especially younger, subordinate males. The function of this relationship is unclear, but it is complex and long-term. On the sandbank, these two species are neighbors and individuals likely know and recognize each other. They display a continuum of behaviors ranging from cooperation to competition.

One of the most interesting observations is that young, maturing female spotted dolphins baby-sit young bottlenose calves. Interspecific baby-sitting has been observed in only a few other areas in the world and illustrates the complex and intimate overlap in the world of these two species of dolphin.

Interspecific Associations

Spotted dolphins in the Bahamas interact regularly with bottlenose dolphins in the area. During these interactions, spotted dolphins often coordinate their sounds and behavior when chasing bottlenose dolphins out of the area. Although many of their interactions are cooperative or neutral, one of the most dramatic displays during interspecific aggression is when bottlenose dolphins dominate and bully spotted dolphins, sometimes physically striking them.

Maturing female spotted dolphins are occasionally observed tending or baby-sitting bottlenose calves (top left). To date, these observations are one way.

On rare occasions, we witness mixed species foraging activity (top right).

A frequently observed mixed species activity is copulation and side-mounting dominance behavior between males of both species (bottom left). The bottlenose dolphins are physically dominant over the spotted dolphins and inflict hard strikes during head-to-head aggressive encounters (bottom right).

57

Social Learning and Intelligence

One of the most fascinating, yet least understood, aspects of the lives of wild dolphins is how they learn what they need to know in life. Dolphins have large and complex brains, live in multifaceted societies, and interact with each other and their neighbors in complex ways. So how do dolphins learn about their world and how intelligent are they?

Dolphins are capable of complex problem-solving and can understand the syntax and semantic aspects of artificial languages. Dolphins also have specialized senses, especially in hearing and in the production of sound. But dolphins can also be very visual, especially species that live in clear waters. Dolphins can use their vision and sound equally to discriminate objects through cross-modal perception. This skill may help in the location and identification of buried prey items in the sand.

Identifying the actual mechanisms of learning are quite challenging. Atlantic spotted dolphins are good candidates for intelligence and social learning. First, dolphins have long lives, giving them time to spend learning about their environment and exploring social relationships. Second, dolphin calves have extended childhoods. In the case of spotted dolphins, they stay with their mothers for 3-5 years, and then go on to spend another 4-5 years in juvenile subgroups. This leaves plenty of time to be exposed to a world of strategies and behaviors conducive towards survival. Third, they live in mixed age and multi-generational groups. This means that there are many opportunities for learning from their mother, peers, and other adults in the society. All these factors add up to the likelyhood that learning and teaching are critical in this society.

Although we can test certain sensory and cognitive abilities in experimental situations, it is in the wild where we will observe how they actually use their brain power to solve the day-to-day challenges of an aquatic life.

Trimy and Duet learn to spar as juveniles, using play threats and mock fighting signals (top left). Play, such as exchanging bits of sargassum, may be an important bonding process between Little Hali and Rosebud (top right).

A hold-down on the bottom may be a disciplinary signal used by the group to warn an individual that his/her behavior is inappropriate (bottom left). Observational learning may be an important process, and during fishing expeditions juveniles can observe successful hunts and catches (bottom right).

59

Unique to a few places in the world, interspecific interactions with humans, if ethically and carefully approached, may give us insight into the complex minds and relationships of dolphins. To safely interact with a potential non-human culture, we must respect and honor their space and behavior, as a species, first and foremost. Only then should we look for an appropriate window within which to interact. "In their world, on their terms" remains our motto for this reason (opposite page).

An emerging, benign, technique for extracting DNA from dolphins and whales is in the collection (top) and processing of fecal material. Regular identification of defecating dolphins (bottom) allows us to collect material and address questions of paternity and population structure.

As I write this book, we prepare for our 19th field season in the Bahamas. My original goal was to spend at least 20 years in the field. I felt such a commitment was necessary to begin to understand and interpret not only the communication system of wild dolphins, but also their larger lives over the many generations and families. As many other researchers have discovered, 20 years seems only a beginning. Now I look to the next additional 20 years to really peel back the layers of complexity of spotted dolphin society in the wild. As time goes by and databases grow, so does our team of colleagues, graduate students, and volunteers. New minds and eyes on both old and new data bring a freshness and richness to any field, and ours is no different.

In this new millennium, we seek to continue not only the regular observations and data collection techniques, but also look forward to using new cutting-edge technologies to illuminate the details of dolphin life. Concomitant with new technology come new paradigms. Can we look with fresh eyes at dolphins in the wild now that we know their identification marks, their relationships, and their communication signals? Can we begin to look at the complexity of these interactions with bigger questions that haunt us about dolphins such as: How do they use their large brains in the wild? Do they have unique ways of communicating with each other or with us? Can we stretch our imaginations and put all our numbers and data together to answer some of the larger mysteries of dolphin life and the dolphin mind? We certainly hope so, and the Wild Dolphin Project is committed to doing just that, perhaps for an additional 20 years. Dolphins and weather permitting, that is!

*Even after 18 years,
I remain amazed and
awed by this society of
dolphins, as individuals
and as family groups.
Their tolerance of us,
and remarkable and
continued curiousity
allows us to continue
our work for the future.
They are truly ambassa-
dors of their world
(opposite page).*

SCIENTIFIC ARTICLES

Au, W.W. L., Lammers, M.O., and Aubauer, R. (1999) A Portable Broadband Data Acquisition System for Field Studies in Bioacoustics. Marine Mammal Science, 15 (2): 526-531.

Bayer, J.B. (2001) An Underwater Analysis of the Behavioral Development of Free-Ranging Atlantic Spotted Dolphin Calves (Birth to 4 Years of Age). Masters Thesis. Florida Atlantic University, 53 pp.

Brunnick, B.J. (2000) The Social Organization of the Atlantic Spotted Dolphin, *Stenella frontalis,* in the Bahamas. Ph.D. Dissertation, Union Institute Graduate School, 149 pp.

Herzing, D.L. (1996) Vocalizations and Associated Underwater Behavior of Free-Ranging Atlantic Spotted Dolphins, *(Stenella frontalis),* and Bottlenose Dolphins, *(Tursiops truncatus).* Aquatic Mammals, 22 (2): 61-79.

Herzing, D.L. (1997) The Natural History of Free-Ranging Atlantic Spotted Dolphins, *(Stenella frontalis)*: Age Classes, Color Phases, and Female Reproduction. Marine Mammal Science, 13 (4): 576-595.

Herzing, D.L. (2000) Acoustics and Social Behavior of Wild Dolphins: Implications for a Sound Society. pp. 225-272 in: *Hearing by Whales and Dolphins.* Au, W.W.L., Popper, A.N., and Fay, R.R. eds. New York, Springer.

Herzing, D.L. and Brunnick, B.J. (1997) Coefficients of Association of Reproductively Active Female Atlantic Spotted Dolphins, *(Stenella frontalis).* Aquatic Mammals, 23 (3): 155-162.

Herzing, D.L. and Johnson, C.M. (1997) Interspecific Interactions Between Atlantic Spotted Dolphins *(Stenella frontalis)* and Bottlenose Dolphins *(Tursiops truncatus)* in the Bahamas, 1985-1995. Aquatic Mammals, 23 (2): 85-99.

Herzing, D.L. and White, T.J. (1999) Dolphins and the Question of Personhood. Etica & Animali Special Issue, 9/98: 64-84.

Marten, K., Herzing, D.L., Poole, M., and Newman Allman, K. (2001) The Acoustic Predation Hypothesis: Linking Underwater Observations and Recordings During Odontocete Predation and Observing the Effects of Loud Impulsive Sounds on Fish. Aquatic Mammals, 27 (1): 56-66.

Moewe, K. (2001) The Social Development of Free-Ranging Atlantic Spotted Dolphins *(Stenella frontalis)* in the Bahamas. Masters Thesis, Florida Atlantic University, 77 pp.

Parsons, K. (2001) Molecular Ecology of Bottlenose Dolphins *(Tursiops truncatus).* Ph.D. Dissertation, University of Aberdeen. Scotland.

Rossbach, K.A. and Herzing, D.L. (1997) Underwater Observations of Benthic Feeding Bottlenose Dolphins, *(Tursiops truncatus),* Near Grand Bahama Island, Bahamas. Marine Mammal Science,13 (3): 498-504.

Rossbach, K.A. and Herzing, D.L. (1999) Inshore and Offshore Bottlenose Dolphin *(Tursiops truncatus)* Communities Distinguished by Association Patterns, Near Grand Bahama Island, Bahamas. Canadian Journal Zoology, 77: 581-592.

MAGAZINE ARTICLES

Whalewatcher, Journal of the American Cetacean Society, Volume 24, No. 3, 1990. "Underwater and Close Up with
     Spotted Dolphins," by Denise L. Herzing. Pp. 16-19.
BBC Wildlife, Volume 9, No. 10, October, 1991. "Dances with Dolphins," by Denise Herzing. Pp. 689-693.
Sonar, Magazine of the Whale and Dolphin Conservation Society, No. 6, Autumn, 1991. "Dolphin Spotting,"
     by Denise Herzing. Pp. 8-10.
Whalewatcher, Journal of the American Cetacean Society, Volume 26, No. 1, 1992. "Family, Friends, and Neighbors,"
     by Denise Herzing. Pp. 13-15.
National Geographic, Volume 182, No. 3, September, 1992. "Dolphins in Crisis," by Kenneth S. Norris, with photo-
     graphs by Flip Nicklin. Pp. 2-35.
Scientific Computing & Automation, January 1993. "Understanding the Behavioral Biology of Dolphins," by Denise
     Herzing with Andrew Davis. Pp. 29-33.
Ocean Realm, June 1995. "Dolphins," by Denise Herzing, with photographs by Flip Nicklin. Pp. 22-29.

TELEVISION DOCUMENTARIES

"Trials of Life" 1991. BBC Series on Wildlife.

"Dolphins: Close Encounters" 1992. From the Nature series on U.S. public television. Hosted by George Page.
     A Wolfgang Bayer Production in association with Thirteen/WNET and Granada Television, Ltd.

"Swimming with Denise" 1993. NHK of Japan, Directed by Seido Hino.

"World of Wonder" 1994. (Segment) Hosted by astronaut Mae Jemison. Discovery Channel.

"Dolphin Dreaming" 1994. From the Natural Neighbors series. Produced by Mark Jacobs.

"Dolphins, with Robin Williams" 1995. From the 'In the Wild' Series. Available from PBS, 1-800-334-3337.

"Dolphin Diaries" 1996. From the BBC Series Natural World. Narrated by Lord David Attenborough. Aired on
     U.S. Public Television. Not available for sale, but frequently rerun on local PBS stations.

"Touched by a Dolphin & Tribes of Sea" 1998. ABC-Kane Production. Domestic and international versions.

"Talking with Aliens" 1999. Pioneer Productions. Narrated by Robin Ellis. Written and directed by Richard Burke-Ward.
     Channel Four Television and TLC.

"Tamzin Outhwaite Goes Wild with Dolphins" 2002. BBC.